Suppose Muscle
Suppose Night
Suppose This In August

Danielle Zaccagnino

Mason Jar Press | Baltimore, MD

suppose it was actual, suppose the mean way to state it was occasional, if you suppose this in August and even more melodiously, if you suppose this even in the necessary incident of there certainly being no middle in summer and winter, suppose this and an elegant settlement a very elegant settlement is more than of consequence

—Gertrude Stein
Tender Buttons

Suppose Muscle
Suppose Night
Suppose This In August

WORRY / OTHERWORLDLY

HOME: girls just wanna have fun on the stereo and mom off-key and me drawing on my skin in marker and an uncle staying on the couch and pop staying on the couch and an aunt living in the back room and a rosary hanging next to a tiny disco ball.

HOME: hair pulling and rollerblading and eating icing out of the jar and my friend hits me with a metal bat by accident and my friend drops a bowling ball on my toes and everyone says i'm a crybaby it's not that serious.

HOME: my stoop and a boom box singalong and dad yelling at the neighborhood kids, they made fun of me, and me apologizing to them, i don't want them to be mad. and dad's face at the screen door, i don't want him to be mad, i don't want anyone to be mad. and i'm not sleeping i just need to close my eyes for a second.

IMAGINE: my head a lightbulb / with a circuit of tongues / flicking and flickering /

HOME: block party karaoke and pushing my aunt up and down the ramp, i like the heaviness of the wheelchair, she likes the ride, and flintstones push-up pops and an above-ground swimming pool and an uncle eating grass for laughs.

HOME: chicken parm and someone's raising their voice and everyone's on edge and sprinklers and getting color and just a warning, fuckface is dropping by, and mister softee and the aid won't do her job and the aid quit again and shut up already would you and 25-cent bracelets on bracelets on bracelets.

HOME: a small room with a slanted roof and everyone is shouting and my hands on my ears and trying to catch my breath and gasping and dripping snot and replaying the cry in the bathroom when everyone falls asleep because i need to feel it again and gasping and shaking because it feels so strong.

IMAGINE: my hair in flames / crackling under the salon's big blow dryer and everyone / roasting marshmallows over / my head and it's distracting / and i close my eyes in a fire daze / and my towel falls like teeth in a dream

HOME: practicing for dance recitals and someone cartwheels into the christmas tree and anisette cookies and an uncle shouting in the street, which neighbors are out, i want so bad to be liked.

HOME: a small playground at night, dad's neighborhood. pink green and blue lanterns, black railings. bocce ball courts with teams of old men. warm air. thick-crust pizza. stray cats. sticky fingers.

HOME: annoyed faces in photos and easter bonnets and my friend starts a circus and i'm a girl with no lines and no moves and i can't breathe in grandma's bed because the boys made fun of me again and my body hair and my jiggling and i can't breathe but i can warble.

IMAGINE: a waterfall / my piano fingers / cupping it like a flame / or framing it on a wall / a rainbowfall /

IMAGINE: snowflakes / 8x10, falling / on a log, floating / on a river i've never seen /

HOME: mom says if i eat too much i'll be roly poly and she'll roll me down the street but i eat jesus at a church and fun dip all the time and bet pennies on pokeeno on grandma's plastic tablecloth and i split maple seeds and stick them to my nose like moth wings or apple shavings and the boys smear fireflies on the street.

HOME: i spin in circles in pink leggings under jean shorts and i love nana's long purple witch-nails and i pray at every grave and i color very carefully and i trip up stairs and i chip my tooth and i crawl into couches like a dust mite.

HOME: my favorite cat dies in a fridge at the flower shop and my street is named after pigeons and i spend days with paranoid squirrels and mom wakes up scared and asks where's the man, was there a man in here, and does it all the time.

IMAGINE: an accordion / whose middle droops / hits the floor as the music / continues, warped

IMAGINE: my body blue / with paint, red / darts shooting / from my eyes / black and endless

HOME: i hold my pillow like a violin and i'm mortified once i say that grandma's butt is like meatballs and i want to do everything right so my page is covered in flecks of rubber and i throw it out anyway because you can see i erased and my teacher says erasing's not allowed.

IMAGINE: me, a whale wriggling / up spray-painted stairs / rorschach cardboard / an ink blot / slipping slipping

IMAGINE: me, swinging / on a grandfather clock like a hammock

HOME: ring pops and candy dots and so much shouting and crouching behind the couch with my sister and so much shouting and hiding in the closet and climbing back down a diving board.

IMAGINE: climbing up the body / of a slick gold trophy / clambering to the clawfoot tub / at the top / where i'll bathe in blankets / if i make it up /

Wilderness Survival Guide, From Memory

You already know about bears, but don't underestimate the shrews. Flash floods are a signal for help. Never leave a sailing stone unattended. Bullet ants are edible; tarantula hawks are not. Gray clouds are a reminder of your mortality. A dust devil can scare away dangerous animals. Keep an exploding tree in your pocket at all times. Fear is a normal reaction. Quicksand is a sign from God. Space rocks are essential to your survival. A person can die from water in just three days.

The City That Tries to Sleep but Has Night Terrors

I wanted to lick the calculus
off her crooked
teeth. The city is never not
in puberty and privacy
isn't her strong suit.
She wants to be known, to be left alone.
When she wakes up to shouting,
she puts her ear to the wall.
Grown and still
damaged, she jumps out the window
of a three-family apartment.
She makes love in a graveyard.
Throws out the newspapers,
says her morals keep her warm.
What kind of sick fuck…
Her name is shorthand
for compulsive need to confess.
She'll never outgrow
this humidity. She has no illusions
of rationality. The salty Hudson
sticks to her skin.

MOSAIC

In 1999, the year I start high school, artists Andrew Ginzel and Kristin Jones create *Oculus*. Three hundred mosaics of eyes cover the walls of the World Trade Center / Park Place / Chambers Street train stations. I don't see them.

In 1999, I'm not allowed underground, not even with a chaperone. I grow up intimidated by the subway, just like my mother does. The way she tells it, the cars are always empty, except for that one lone predator. I want to tell her I will not get raped every time I'm alone, but I don't know if it's true.

In 1999, I go to the Bronx High School of Science on the yellow cheese-bus, and my high school has a mural too. Sixty-three feet tall: Charles Darwin, the Tower of Pisa, a prism, a telescope, Marie Curie, a flask, Archimedes, a screw pump. Underneath it says, "Every great advance in science has issued from a new audacity of imagination." I am not a scientist, and I am not audacious.

In high school, too many eyes are on me. Boys tell me where I place in their rankings, follow me home on the school bus. One writes a screenplay and says I'm the inspiration. The main character cuts himself, carves a girl's name into his arm.

In high school, I keep my head down. I want nothing more than not to be looked at.

Oculus starts with students from Stuyvesant, a high school like mine. Photographs of their eyes.

Eye after eye made of stone, gold, Venetian glass, and marble.

In my junior year, I sign up for a class trip to Italy. On September 11th, my plans are changed; now, planes are more dangerous than anything else.

Oculus exists before 9/11, and it exists after. Then it's thought of as a memorial, when everything is seen through a new lens.

In my senior year, we go to prom at the Plaza, graduation at Lincoln Center. In the 66th Street-Lincoln Center mosaic lives an acrobat, bending back midair with pointed toes and flat hands. Like she's lifting the ground above her, the city. Her body is lithe, elf-like. And a singer, still, regal. Others dancing, flying, building.

But at Chambers Street, one of the eyes looks like it's falling apart. The lid like a sunrise, but the center shattered.

In college I can finally take the train by myself.

My home is near Main Street. In my station, a mosaic by Ik-Joong Kang. This one is above our heads. I can't see it up close, but it looks like a million photo booth pictures. I see a terrarium, I think, and the towers. Smokestacks and masks and planets. Outlines in front of a smeared-color world. *A Happy World.*

Underground, I'm safe. I'm cozy in the crowds. Our bags are checked for bombs.

In college, I take the Q16 to the 7 to the W. The ride to NYU is longer than my night's sleep.

The train is where I nod off every morning, on a stranger's shoulders, on my chest, by accident. Where people fall into my lap and I fall into theirs.

Underground, I run into people I know, people I feel like I know, and people I will never know.

There's so much detail in the eyes. You even see the white of the waterline. Close up there's depth. The marbling of each piece. How they don't line up from tile to tile. Some smooth. Some weathered. Some square, some broken. I like the chipped pieces best.

Another mosaic, at 42nd Street: *The Revelers.* Party hats and noisemakers. Heels and bluish faces. Pastel. Ribbons and white shadows. White shadows merging into each other. Noise and more noise.

Once, a man comes toward me, screaming, almost drooling, his whole body tense and nearing eruption. He says I'm a cunt, I'm a cunt, I'm a fucking cunt. My boyfriend laughs; he has never been in this situation.

Once, a man in a white tracksuit, white sneakers, squeaky clean, stares straight at me while he strokes his erection. We are not the only people in the subway car.

(In *The Death and Life of Great American Cities,* Jane Jacobs writes, "There must be eyes upon the street." For safety and community, you need more people, more looking.)

Once, a man looks at me as I get off the train. He says, "Mmm, there's some fine-looking pussy in this town."

A man pulls down his pants, shits in a paper bag.

A man gets close to me in a crowded car. I'm holding onto a strap above my head. He starts grinding against me. At first I'm not sure if it's happening, but it is. I say stop three times. I cry.

(What Jane calls eyes on the street—do the rules apply underground?—look down at the *Village Voice.*)

The eyes on Chambers Street are fractured. And it's hard not to see them as apathetic. As drooping a little.

In Penn Station, another mosaic, *Circus of Earthly Delights.* An emcee and a fire-eater and a sad clown and what looks like a monstrous spider. And a man's transformation, and wildlife. There's fire all around. This is where you want to be. I promise, it is.

A teacher once asks my class, "What is your place of power?" I think of the subway. I think: a place of powerlessness.

What man lacks in consent, he makes up for in "there was nowhere else to put my hands."

New York hates her trains. Makes them smell like feces.

In one eye, a pupil like a diamond. Another: wide in fear. White and sticky.

Underneath the Brooklyn Museum, another mosaic, gargoyles and busts, on silver and gold. Like a precious artifact on a toilet seat.

When something happens to my friend, I start praying all the time. For each woman I see, a quick prayer to a god I almost forgot.

And a mosaic, too, in Jamaica Station, the smelliest of all stations. I can't focus on what's around me.

They're not people, just images of pieces of people, just tiny tiles with rough edges.

In the Greek myth of Polyphemus, the cyclops is blinded by Odysseus. The hero calls himself Nobody, so the cyclops only shouts that "Nobody" has hurt him.

And another eye: ethereal. A shimmery mermaid green. A speck of turquoise. A tear, or gum chewed up and stuck on.

There's life on the train, more than anywhere else.

And another eye: plainer than others. And another eye: darker and rounder. And another eye: distinctly female. And another eye: reptilian.

And another eye: deep shadows. And another eye, outlined clearly: the skin is red, raw.

And another eye: hypnotic. And another eye: It's had enough.

The kind of person who would fight back.

The muscles around the human eye are called orbicularis oculi. I love the way these words move.

Then there's *Blooming* at the 59th street station. Aside from *Oculus*, it's my favorite, and this one comes with text.

From William Butler Yeats: "In dreams begin responsibility."

From Gwendolyn Brooks: "Conduct your blooming in the noise and whip of the whirlwind."

In this mosaic, there are shoelaces I might trip on. There's red, yellow, green, and blue. A *Wizard of Oz* heel, fallen off and floating, and a cup of coffee that looks like an ocean. Tree branches split like frog toes, and the shine of the tiles.

Good Girl With a Hammer

I'm the one I buried deep
in hand-stitched pocks of earth

The threat of birth, like the thread of death,
continues to force my hand

Good girl in the dirt, eager to please
Good girl in the rafters

When all you have is shame
everything looks like a hammer

but there's something to be said for that sensation

Dear diplomat, dear daughter,
when has devotion ever been perfect?

Who can write a whole song by heart?
I've had enough near-misses to last a lifetime

So read my lips like a prayer card
Saint of knobby knees and twist-turned feet:

Swing hard
Swing loose

And if you find me making
too many commands, understand it
as a groping for power
as a momentary lapse
of self-consciousness

Celebrate
that small triumph

Good Girl With a Habit

it was the first time they'd seen fire
she put it in her mouth

a glowing touchstone, shy violet
pawing at the past

she asked the world which still loved her
who still loved her

spiked with pine, champagne, fever
on a rooftop she was one of many

holed and held in, gilded

they lived in the flood times
they talked about adding value

a study in ballet, in waves
the tiny vicious things on their tongues

EDIBLES: A PRIMER

i. On Acuity

I could spend my first time in a gondola, at the Van Gogh Museum, or on cobblestone streets, but I love nothing more than privacy and I choose the hotel room. I share a bed and a brownie packed with THC with a girl I barely know. A waif with graham cracker hair. There's a movie on TV—Brad Pitt as Death personified. It takes a long time, but when it hits, there's no mistaking it. Every second starts to stretch. Each muscle makes itself known. The night has a strawberry glow. Death, his girlfriend, and her father are still on the screen, but I'm confused. It's their prosody. I ask, *Are they all slam poets?* Her eyes, swollen shut, overflow at an equator. As she laughs, the box spring creaks.

ii. On Measuring

I'm curled up in a ball on my foam IKEA mattress. There's a zipper along the side. Sometimes I stroke it when I'm feeling anxious, but not right now. Right now, there's a war on U.S. soil. I don't know the particulars, and there's no room for them anyway. My body lurches in that way it does before I vomit, but there is no such relief. It stays hypertonic. *They're gonna kill us all.* My boyfriend, Ben, climbs the ladder to my lofted bedroom, a plywood structure that can't be trusted with stacks of books, and puts his hands firmly on my face. *We're in your apartment on Eldert Street,* he says, to orient me. *Brooklyn. Everyone is okay.* He tells me what happened. We poured cannabutter oil on my mock chicken. There's a party on the roof above us. Hundreds of people are up there, walking, dancing, drunkenly stumbling, and every few seconds new fireworks burst. I convulse and he grips my arms. *It's not a war,* he repeats. *It's the Fourth of July.* We poured the oil freely, to make sure it would work.

iii. On The Buddy System

The tall one won't stop staring. He's trying to read my expression. The shorter one is inching closer. I'm in Jersey City with friends of friends, mostly programmers. Around my age. Everyone is telling diving board stories. The shorter one puts his hand on my leg. The hairs on his lip are wet. *How about you?* the tall one asks me, but I can't answer. I don't know how to talk. The movements are too complex and foreign. I realize that I'm not in a group anymore; I'm in a corner with two men. *I bet you understand everything we're saying, huh?* the tall one says. I try to move my head a little. They look at each other. I see my phone. I try to text help.

iv. On Assertion

My neighbor is hosting a party. He divvies up the responsibilities. I'm on haunted house supplies, minus the worms. Park Slope's pet stores are all sold out. My boyfriend bikes around Brooklyn looking for dry ice. A friend makes popcorn balls, each kernel stuck to another by weed-infused caramel. Someone comes through with the worms last minute. All the ingredients for a perfect night. I practice sign language with my boyfriend, for when hands work better than vocal cords. I close all the fingertips of my right hand together, the way my family does to prove a point, and move my hand from chin to cheek. *This means home.* He mimics the gesture. *When I do this, you walk me back.*

v. On Communion

Alone, his hands are ocean. Us and a song, twenty-five minutes long. Don't be distracted. Two people can balloon. Can rise. Can spill like paint, thick, indiscriminate. Console crannies. *It's not so impossible.*

vi. On Depersonalization

I'm in a kitchen. As I look at the person across the table, the room keeps shifting. *Danielle.* Some new reality is created every second, and the scene falls like a set of Polaroids. *Danielle.* The man puts water in front of me. I ask him if my face is moving. I think of asking: *Is this body mine? Who am I?* He looks concerned. My boyfriend comes. I move my hand from chin to cheek.

vii. On Permeability

Everyone is really friendly and I feel confident. A recording plays in the background. It's someone's voice. I'm so free today I could probably do a dance recital and not fuck it up. The voice continues, and I realize it's me. I don't know what I'm saying. Like with stroke survivors, some things are automatic. The alphabet, for example. I examine the faces looking back attentively. I try to figure out if I've told any secrets, if they can hear what I'm thinking—they nod their heads enthusiastically—who, if anyone, I've insulted—their skin is smoother than I thought—and whether or not they've earned my intimacy. The voice sounds happy.

viii. On Amplification

It starts in an ovary, or maybe both. There are strains for pain. Clearly this isn't one of them. It travels around my hips toward my coccyx; down my thighs, spear-tipped. Loud. A hangman stick figure, stiff, I worship the moments between memory.

ix. On Reframing

I scarf down a summer supper. Watermelon, falafel, grainy garden burgers. I eat a cookie someone baked that morning. Hours go by. A bust. I try another. Flooded, I hit capacity. Skin, sounds, whirl, shutdown. This time I know what to do. These are the words: *I need to sleep.* I find the girl I want to hear them. She walks me to her room and I lock the door. I lie awake but breathe easy alone. I don't know who I am, and who cares? Electrical impulses are firing everywhere, my body the carnival grounds. I grin under the covers and let my limbs jump.

x. On Knowing What You're Getting

Driving back from Seattle's first dispensary, New Year's Eve, I suck on skunky cinnamon candy. Five milligrams, sativa. The buzz is playground gentle, spinning in circles. Two hours turn it into a body high. My shoulders drop. My boyfriend fries spinach while his dad tries a hybrid. He shows me old pictures (cheeks low and pale beneath a bowl cut), swivels slightly in a computer chair. The family mills around. I take a shower with lemon shampoo. Yellow fills the room.

Horoscopes for Women Like Me

Think of evergreens. Keep trying.

You'll find the hours full
of pinprick patter. You won't know
your own stench.

Imagine yourself floating
bowlegged and numb.

You'll find celestial bodies
will always be manhandled.

You'll find your mother's and all mothers' bones
dangling on rows of rope and you'll wonder
if that tibia twitching is hers.

You won't know.

You'll dig your own warren. Keep crawling
until dirt swallows sound.

You'll find you're only one person.

When your head flies off in the storm,
your knees will wince in sympathy.

Constantly practice
distortion of perspective.

When you confuse yourself
with someone else, stay there.

Even blades of grass will bicker.
Live in the sky.

Introduction to Trepanation

we are the new neutrals, a pop
of trepanation

though drinking your name
something's cartoon about you

we're splitting our seams
trying to show our work

a fennec in a snowstorm
an almost balanced equation

two: times I thought the moon
would crash into me   come barreling
       through my windshield

instinct blankness: save me
from who I was and am

I fear a metaphor has taken me
away from you—I worry sometimes

I'll never be loved enough

CARNAGE DREAMS AND *TWIN PEAKS*

My anxious mind is an endless reel of torture porn*, a buffet of body horror.

> <*a genre of pure
> gratuitous gore. see also:
> splatter, splatstick, gorno>

(For years I believed a teenager slit my sister's throat. I didn't look for the scar or confirm the memory with any member of my family. The assault was, to me, a given of our upbringing.)

(My other recurring dream: my father crawled out of a sewer, night after night, covered in bruises, looking to me for help.)

(Now my brain is like a greedy socialite; it won't reuse the same dark fantasy twice.)

(In another dream, a stranger broke in to strangle me.)

> (At a gas station, tried to choke me out, knocked me
> unconscious against a wall.)

[[My favorite show is *Twin Peaks*.]]

[[Like my friend, Laura Palmer was raped
by her father. And just like in real life,
no one could see
who he was, including me.]]

[[a demon named Bob]]

[[a mystery that was never meant to be solved]]

<Psychologists call these
intrusive images.>

(a tongue like chunks
have been bitten out)

(I tried to escape a killer by strangling him with a wire, like Audrey
Horne in a back room at One-Eyed Jack's. His neck was too thick,
or my wire the wrong kind. The dream was nonlinear. I tried
hiding, climbing out the window, an Uber to Detroit. In every
do-over, I died.)

<Is it frustrating to read
the contents of my mind?>

Don't worry. There are bright pockets too.

[a freewrite: how do I explain this to you? / put your hand
to my forehead / a pink leather dinosaur / zipped up club

kid / derby girls rolling roughshod around a sticky rink / a peacock sea / a Barbie balloon in Ken county]

(Michael Alig cut apart Angel's body, stuffed it in a trunk.)

(A rigid blade sliced through my body the way Gordon Ramsay filets a fish.)

[[*Twin Peaks* is a master class
in balance]]

[a freewrite: a wrestler in a wedding veil / a jalopy / a gun turns out to be a fish / the moon is like a baby the earth pushed out / cauliflower clouds / salt & pepper shaker rain / if we put half of my brain / with half of yours / what would happen?]

[a kissing booth / dark dirt & croissants / a gingerbread man, his honey-filled brow / a carnival chorus in a red shimmy dress / carbonated flash word salad & where we've sailed]

[gold figurines / in game shows & stirring sauce / buried in your spaghetti, a little whale / i want three lives, or four / but i would settle for two]

[a dizzy-eyed bird with a lopsided crown / vandalize the mountain sculpture / make it up with lipstick]

<Has the pendulum swung
                           too far? I'm just trying
                           to get by.>

[[My favorite character is Nadine. She lost her eye
after a honeymoon buckshot accident, suffered a
loveless marriage, attempted suicide, but
underneath all that, she was full
of pure joy. Glass-crushing, milkshake-loving,
cheerleader/wrestler, man-throwing Nadine.]]

[[though Bob is the reason I watch]]

(A copper wire in my chest. I tried to pull it out without
breaking off pieces of bone. He lifted it up and it caught
on the thyroid cartilage, the central ridge that we see as
an Adam's apple.)

(Someone lured me into a warehouse party, a therapeutic
experiment, "radical inclusion." Once you're there, you
have to take part. Trapped in a room, I heard screams. My
best friend in a closet. I was next. They told me I had to
take a drug, a brown sticker in the shape of a circle. I stuck
it on someone else, a bald man, and ran down a staircase. A
rape dungeon. The only way to escape was to take over the
game. It had to keep going; only the roles would change.
I had to stay focused.)

I've never been a violent person. I've never been in a physical fight, and I would run if offered the chance, but I'm unashamed of my thoughts.

<I'm just trying
to be less intrusive
to my images.>

When I was ashamed of them, I avoided them. When I avoided them, there were compulsions, there was fuzzy, circular thinking, a drain on my resources.

[[In defense of violence on TV: How else would I feel normal?]]

The effort it takes to block thoughts out is much greater than the effort it takes to process them, though processing them sometimes seems unbearable. Darkness is like an upside-down puzzle. I can't get started until I find its borders.

<It's not safe to simplify
so much that you suppress
your fears
or your ability to get past them.>

[a dynasty / of bicycle lane raccoons / magma in the shape of a tree / the fluttering wild of an infant drone / my head pops like a megalo-phone / and a dragon flies up through my throat]

[a woman with blank white eyeballs and glitter brows]

(attacked by a fat pterodactyl)

[flying into space first class / a ballerina beams flowers on the stage / builds mountain ranges / on my skin]

I still can't wrap my mind around what humans are really capable of.

(I could name 24 hours of sleep and exactly where to find them.)

[["An evil that great in this beautiful world. Finally, does it matter what the cause?"]]
[["Yes."]]

Fear permeates my subconscious

[everything about tomorrow is a balloon / I love it like a balloon & I live in the balloon / a tickle fight on an eggy night / his buttery butt / makes him slip across the ocean]

but I can sleep inside a tornado.

[I filled out the paperwork for a new job, but in two minutes the office would be taken over by demons from an alternate dimension. I was herded out the door. Soon I realized I hadn't even turned in the forms. I needed to get back there before it was too late. Agent Cooper worked out a deal: the manager would let me back in and Cooper would fight one of the demon men. He treated the creatures like friends, but he chose the one he was a little less fond of. There was some punching, Cooper was thrown on the ground. Then the demon peed on him, crazed and giddy, a stream that made a wild arc in the air and seemed to last forever. Cooper shot an electric bolt straight up the middle of the monster's body, like zipping up a human suit. Everyone agreed that was the winning move. Cooper apologized to the man he didn't choose. A little girl offered the dejected demon a puppy. The tree topped with a brain was there. I was so happy I got to see it in real life.]

I'm giving up on performing wellness, work that tired me more than it helped me.

(Trapped on an aircraft. My captors were watching. I begged my neighbor, carve my secrets into bone, the underside of my scapula. No one would see but I'd still have written them.)

(Fists shaking. Powerless all over again. Something like a panic attack. Bobby Briggs punched my mother in the face. Nobody believed me. My husband is trying to wake me, he pulls my eyelids open, but it keeps going. Her bruised cheekbone. Blue and the wrong angle. This has never happened before. I've never been filled with so much violent need.)

[& eyelids under those eyelids / eyelids all the way down]

[["Where's Bob now?"]]

Now When I Hear Body Farm

It's just a laboratory. Instead of Bunsen burners,
they stock up on limbs, learn about decay. How bodies change
under aberrant conditions. How to tell time-since-death.

Two hours, she told me through a text.

Now when I hear "body farm," I see [W][M]
half in the ground, arms out.
A scarecrow with pinpoint

pupils, a blue smile, he starts to grow
toward vultures, decompose.
Here it's business

as usual. I can see the man—
straw hat, red and denim, spitting
but graceful—shoot skag into the soil,
scatter pills like seeds.

It's just a lab. Stick to data:
Who collects the bodies?
And how long do they keep them?

What are the odds
that a bottle of pills
would empty by accident?

And what kind of man
would grow a friend dead?
And will this soil ever be wet?

Heroisch is German for powerful.

Now when I hear "heroine"
she's telling the children
(not too much at once)

Now when I hear [   ]
Now body, now blue

Now when I hear "tolerance"
how much of ourselves we can take
Now free, now base

Now when boy is moon rock
I blood-brain barrier

Now when I body

Now when I farm body
I call it [   ]

Now straw, now barn
Now sing a digging song

Dig boy, dig moon
Pupil pill-point
Needle blue

Now when dog bite vein
Now when plaid shoot soil

What kind of man
On the body farm

Now heart
Now method

Now body

Now blue

Billboard

I know you know the armor
I slap together some nights:
woman blown up & billboarded
stud-pierced & ghost-smoking,
an ad for arrogance & cocktails

beneath I'm a combination
of my aunt & a zombie & johnny depp
at the end of cry-baby. burst
blood vessels, lily liver, shallow

breathing, trying to remove
all distancing phrases. throughout history
I've been scared of scope and scale. let's table it.

I can't bear much time
in the limelight, rind soaked
in vodka, I'm death-burned
& feedstock. open your books

to page eleven. sometimes
I have to lift my breasts to breathe.
sometimes I dream myself untoothed
in a nursery, filling my pockets
with pureed peas & spaghetti sauce.

THE MISSING LINK

"Nobody's from here except the Ice Man," the man behind me said. I was on the 16D in Minneapolis and I couldn't remember where I was supposed to get off. The man behind me was from Senegal, and he was talking to a younger guy from Taiwan. I was from Queens, New York, and I hated the Midwest.

I never meant to move there. I was only there for Ben's career, and I was starting to resent it. And I was nearly positive I missed my stop. I got confirmation a few minutes later when the driver pulled over and turned off the engine. It was then I realized I was the only passenger still on the bus. "How far is it to 27th?" I asked. I figured I would walk back in the direction we came from. "Far," she answered. "Just stay on the bus and we'll go around again." She left the bus for a smoke break and, trying to forget my embarrassment, I returned to the Ice Man. Was that a Minnesotan myth or just a figure of speech? I asked the internet while I waited.

First, it told me that Bobby Drake was a mutant in the X-Men, known for encasing his enemies in a block of ice, which I knew. His powers were so out of his control that he needed a belt to quell them, and it was hard not to imagine it as a chastity belt. He was born in Port Washington, Long Island, near the college I attended my freshman year, where I studied linguistics. Or was that Port Jeff? Either way, this was not the Ice Man they were talking about.

Richard Kuklinski was a hitman for the Mafia. He was convicted of five murders but probably responsible for dozens more. He killed for other reasons, too: to get back at a bully, for instance, and to get exercise. He disposed of the bodies in many ways, such as feeding them to gigantic cave rats, and freezing them to prevent anyone from determining the time of death. Kuklinski was from Dumont, New Jersey. Not the right guy, but I was a little happy to stumble across another East Coaster.

Oetzi, also called the Man from Hauslabjoch, was born in 3300 BCE, near the Alps. Ice had both crushed and preserved his body. He had 61 tattoos in all. I had, at this time, eight. I would probably never catch up. He wore a leather loincloth and his intestines were full of chamois, deer, and bread. I had been a vegetarian for nine years, and none of this was relevant.

My search had to get more specific. "Minnesota Ice Man." There he was: no picture, but an explanation. A Neanderthal, a "missing link," or, most likely, a hoax. A State Fair sideshow exhibit of a man frozen in a block of ice. Not as satisfying as I'd hoped, but then again, neither was the State Fair. I had gorged myself, the prior summer, on fried Oreos and pizza-on-a-stick and had gone home sick. The Fair was one of those things Minneapolitans were most proud of, and it was utterly regrettable. Me and the city just never clicked.

The bus was re-peopled, and we started moving again, and I had to be more vigilant this time. I knew what he had meant anyway, the man behind me, when he said, as I got lost in my resentment and the streets of the cold, disconnected city, "Nobody's from here except the Ice Man. And if we stay here long enough, we'll all become Ice People, too."

Sounds or Mountains?

I'm bodiless, trivial,

two footholds, steady but distant
settling down in a ghost town

(a flare-up)

I'm built for hard times
confused in the sunshine

pupal or paperweight
pierce or puncture

everyone is someone I've met before
and I didn't like them the first time

a lightbulb pops in place of my skull
what happens next?

Autobiography of an Oddity

Let me name the impulse: to minimize
discomfort. To feel the skin.

The subject is nature. To fry
what's frozen, drip honey
on a block of milk.

To punctuate a world that doesn't belong to me.

I would squeeze myself
through any doorway, trying
to come out the right person.

And to maximize it too:

The subject is will. To bludgeon a landscape.
A burst of happiness (arrogance), a dragon-need
and knowing where to go.

All the words in the correct order.
Going to the market, catching them at the very last minute.

I would smile myself into
and out of every situation
fast, pretending to be ready.

When I said burn I meant sleep. Please just let me sleep.

The subject is time. I was caught
unaware. Trying to swipe a little treasure.

I filled my tires up with snow. There were times
it was quiet enough.

TOUCH, AND A FRACTURING

In a sultry-red room, a stranger dragged a stone, smooth and heavy, across my neck. Worried the heat would escape quickly, I pointed her toward a ropy muscle. I was intoxicated by incense, instrumentals, and oxytocin. And touch. It was our wedding anniversary. Ben and I were spending it in Lutsen, Minnesota. I remember thinking that my muscles must have been permanently changed. I wanted to spend every day in this room, in this routine. It reminded me of reading a book so good it made me want to be a writer.

A woman comes in at nine. A holster holding a bottle of lotion sits on my hip. I usually use the one labeled apricot, grapeseed, and sesame. I spread it on her skin in broad strokes. She tells me I have a good touch. She says there's something special about it. Some people just don't have that. I wonder what she means as I knead her legs like dough, losing myself in the motion. Petrissage. I love a calf that fits in my hands. The main muscle, the gastrocnemius, bifurcates into a medial and a lateral head. I spread them apart several times before squeezing them back together. Deep to this is the soleus, which I reach while lifting her ankle. Some scientists believe that the soleus and the gastroc are one singular muscle.

Now I'm in San Marcos, Texas. I was accepted into an MFA program in creative writing. Ben stayed behind to finish his PhD.

A man comes in at one. His back is hurting, which is not a surprise. He's built, and his shoulders hunch slightly forward. He lifts weights. *Your pecs spend a lot of time contracting,* I explain, as I pull his arm to the side, supine, put one foot forward and lunge into him, sinking my weight into the pectoralis minor through my palm. He's shocked. *You're strong for a girl your size.*

Most nights I can't sleep. Ben would say I have shpilkes. A Yiddish word for nervous energy. At home he always tried to convince me to come to bed early, but even then I wouldn't be sleeping, I'd be jumping on the mattress or biting him, yipping, wanting him to wake up and play. The only touch that helps my anxiety is a hard touch. Grazing would make it much worse. *Push me down,* I'd ask. *Lie on top of me. I might be up all night. Your full weight,* I'd remind him. I don't know why he held himself up. I always wanted the full weight.

A woman comes in at three. Her muscles ache. I warm her up with effleurage before going for the deep tissue. *Deeper,* she says, almost immediately.

Most people think massage therapy is meant to be painful, but it should never really hurt. You ease your way into it. You use rhythm and routine to teach the body what to expect. You prepare it with heat. With washcloths, hot stones, warming oil. You ask the client to take deep breaths. I ask her to take a deep breath. *You're not going deep enough,* she says again. I use my fists, my elbows, my angles, lean on the body like a coffee table, letting it hold all my weight, but still, she complains, *you're not getting deep enough.*

Here I'm studying poetry, and there's nobody to lie on me. Here I'm not practicing massage. Here there's nobody to touch. There's memory.

A woman comes in as soon as we open. She always asks for lymphatic drainage, which involves lightly stroking her skin to move lymph—a watery liquid made of interstitial fluid and blood cells which carries the body's waste away— toward ducts by the ears, the jaw, the armpits, and the clavicle. If you feel muscle, you've gone far too deep. I barely touch her in this hour-long, routine slow-tickle. It would drive me up a wall, but it's what she wants. I go slow. Her eyes are limpid. Every week we barely speak, but it feels familial.

In lieu of a human, over a blanket, I pile pillows on top of me every night. The cushions from my couch. My laptop. Textbooks. I cover my stomach, my thighs, my feet. Like stones. Like a paperweight. I'm too flimsy without it. There's a video game I used to play called *Katamari Damacy*. The protagonist tries to reconstruct the skies. He rolls and grows his magical ball by picking up anything it will stick to. Bananas, cows, now ladders, whole buildings. The king is always let down by his haul. He wants something bigger, heavier. In lieu of a blanket, I pile lamps on top of me. My dressers, the fridge. I cover my face, my hands. A mattress, a box spring. A parking garage, a campus. Katamari means "clump" or "clod." Damacy means "soul." Bigger, heavier. It's never enough.

A woman comes in at four. I look over her intake form. So much is missing. I try to get the answers; she lays on the table. I tell her to get undressed. *To your level of comfort,* I add, like I always do. *And get settled under the sheet.* After washing my hands, I knock on the door, and enter. She appears ready, but her sheet is down at her waist. I pull it up to her neck quickly, but she doesn't seem embarrassed. People want to be vulnerable here.

Carmen Gimenez Smith says in one of her poetry collections, "I silence the brain with language play." I don't know if silence is the right word.

Spasms, deliriums: madness is such a female world, but that's just my take. –*Milk and Filth* / Clouds are almost entirely made up of milk; that is why they are white. We too are more than 90 percent milk. –*The Melancholy of Anatomy* / And at that moment our embrace was broken by our fall to the Moon's surface, where we rolled away from each other among those cold scales. —*Cosmicomics* / A paragraph is a time and place, not a syntactic unit. —*My Life* /] for me away from —*If Not, Winter*

> A woman comes in at noon. Her daughter is with her, running circles around the table. The woman takes off her shirt while I interview her about her aches, with the door still open. She's wearing a black bra with no underwire. Her daughter is unfazed by the familiar sight. I hear footsteps in the hallway and shut the door. They don't speak English, so I hold up the sheet to give to the mother. She sits and presses my hand into her back. She moans. Contrary to popular belief, this job is not sexual, but it is intimate. The daughter is drawn in by her mother's pain. She climbs onto the table and presses her hand over mine. She smiles at me shyly. I show her to push with the bottom of her palm, not her fingers. *Good,* her mother says.

The beauty of fragmentation in poetry, defined by Edward Hirsch as having "a part broken off, something cut or detached from the whole, something imperfect," is that it reflects the mind. My mind, divorced from a body, craves shape. Constraint. My thesis advisor asks about my philosophy on fragmentation—I ask if she's referring to lines that are disjunctive in style/thought (does Prufrock dare disturb, etc.) or fractures created by white space, ungrammatical breaks on the page, and she says either or both—and I don't have one, or at least I don't think I do. It just feels right. I see Ben once a month. I'm not citing that as an influence on my poetry. Like

I said, I don't shy away from—can discursive be used as a noun? The MFA is like a cerebral summer camp for dysfunctional adults. The day is split into reading, writing, workshopping, and reflecting. I feel no obligation to participate in the physical world.

A man comes in at eight. He's in town from Portland, recently divorced. He tells me right away. *She cheated,* he adds, as I work on his triceps. He's lying face up, with his arms hooked behind the head of the table. *And then flaunted it on Facebook.* He asks me if I've ever been with a woman. If I'm single. If I have plans that night. I dodge his questions, rub his attachment points. Where muscle connects to bone by tendon. He tells me he has a hotel room. I tell him I have a husband and move on to his biceps. The primary muscle moving in an action is the agonist, the other the antagonist. He says she won't let him see his children. He asks for my number. I work down the arm, squeeze my hand around his.

I'm always dividing my life into segments. In this essay:

when I worked with bodies	with thoughts
when Ben was a body	a voice
when I dwelled in my body	dwelled
when I was touched	& wasn't

A friend comes in at four. She leaves her sheet off
too. People want to be vulnerable here. She leaves
me a note: "You are a goddess."

Writer and translator Jennifer Scappettone says, in the introduction
to *Locomotrix: Selected Poetry and Prose by Amelia Rosselli,* that
"we would be mistaken to conflate the difficulty of this poetry with
psychic difficulty."

A woman comes in at five. I start on her scalp. Her
face is down in the cradle. Her hair falls toward
me, tangled, but more wild than messy. She's had
a lot of headaches lately. I make circles around her
skull and move my fingertips down her neck. You
can't isolate a single part of the body. My teacher
used to compare it to a sweater. When one thread
is pulled, the whole garment gets warped. The
knots in her neck are causing tension in her head.
I spend a long time with each one, working them
loose. I get her to turn over. She doesn't ask what
I'm doing. It takes a lot of trust to put your neck
in someone's hands. I slip my fingers under her
back, slightly cup them, pull the tips up the erector
spinae, the long thick muscles on each side of the
spine, and when I get to the bottom of the head,
the occiput, I hold it, using my fingers as pillars,
and I feel her let something go. I remember Lutsen.

I'm reading four books this weekend, three of them for my thesis
meeting. Sylvia Plath's *Ariel,* Gertrude Stein's *Tender Buttons,* and

Victoria Chang's *The Boss*. I write to my advisor: "Can we talk more about fragmentation? Does it appear in all three? I'm losing my grip on the word." I could make a case for everything as broken.

> A woman comes in at three. She tweaked something. She tells me to get closer to the spine. Closer. She puts my finger on bone. I'm nervous I'll break something. My teacher always said that the bony protuberances on each side can snap off with too much force. I place my hands laterally and move in slowly until I find the trigger point. She lets out a sound of relief.

Bob Perelman refers to Stein, in an online course through ModPo, as an "active difference-making machine." Not in the sense, I think, of her overall impact, but in the room she makes for multiplicity. Tiny splits through semantics. Disruption. My poetry professor said, "We must love disruption to create something." To want to disturb the blank page. In *Tender Buttons,* Stein writes, "If the centre has the place then there is distribution. That is natural. There is a contradiction and naturally returning there comes to be both sides and the centre. That can be seen from the description."

> A man comes in at eleven. He has spent the morning in the sun. As I move my hands across his body, dead skin cells peel off him like a grated gray cheese. Not all intimacy is pretty.

I can guess at *tender* but I wonder why buttons makes it into the title. My advisor said she's heard a theory—I already forget from where; Google pulls up Joshua Schuster quoting Kathryn Kent (2003)—that the title is a play on words, tend her buttons, a secret nod to her lover. In a letter to the *New York Review of Books* in 1971, Paul Padgette states that "tender buttons" are obviously nipples, and the reviewer, Virgil Thomson shouldn't beat around the bush. Thomson objects, noting that, for one, although the title may be "a bilingual pun from the French *tendres boutons*," it could refer simply to "the early buddings of a tree or plant," framing it in terms of "a natural force" and "new development." However, he also notes that "there is another erogenous zone in female anatomy that could just as easily be called a tender button."

> A friend comes in at seven. When I get to his
> quads, I tuck the sheet around his legs and place
> the bony edge of my hand at the top of his thigh,
> as high as I will go. He relaxes as soon as I mark
> the boundary.

In my undergraduate neuroanatomy class, we'd all giggle when my professor talked about axon terminals, the tips of dendrites which send out neurotransmitters like serotonin (too little, in my case). Terminal *boutons,* she'd call them, in her French accent. Tender, terminal buttons. The message goes out across the synapse; the neurons don't actually touch.

> A woman comes in at six. She has pain between
> her ribs. I slide my fingers along each one, dipping
> into the spaces between them. There is nothing
> more intimate than contact with the intercostals,
> the muscles that help us breathe and cough and

laugh, a part of the body that rarely knows touch. It takes trust. I want to have this experience with everyone I know.

"I write for the still-fragmented parts in me, trying to bring them together." – Adrienne Rich

When we read Sappho, we have to reconcile with the gaps where her words were burned. Anne Carson's translations emphasize those chasms:

]
]
]
] thought
] barefoot
]
]
]
]

A man comes in at eleven. He wants a full-body massage. He tells me partway through that his feet are killing him. I massage feet the same way every time. I lay my thumbs, from tip to carpometacarpals, flat on the sole of the foot and cup my hands around it. I stretch it apart and hold it there. Wiggle, pull, and warm the toes, trace around the ball of the foot. I push my fist down the sole, from toes to heel, to prevent calcium from building up into spurs. Knuckle the heel, which gets beaten up throughout the day. I move on to the top of the foot and press between the metatarsals. Soothe the ankles. It's amazing how much our feet can take. I approach his, but I'm blown away by the stench. I need to sanitize. The switch from lotion—infused with calming scents for aromatherapy, warm from my hands, which are warm from the body, the movement—to Purell is harsh. Sterile.

I can't stand to look at another book, so I pick up my phone, scroll through my contacts, judge them harshly: do not let in / does not let in / studies in breath / dearth / monogamously alcoholic / the third degree / the ordinary side of a glacier / wants to touch me / might actually try to / disguise as error / error as personality / unwilling to unravel / the talent in seeing / the smell of the ocean / my therapist / by interesting I mean messy / the amplification of embarrassment / years beyond a tune-up / the spin cycle / a plosive / and *only* seeing / always being a little bit scared / living in a body vs. everything else.

Over the span of a week, I put into my body: 280 fluid ounces of Coca-Cola; 16 ounces of Lone Star; 15 milligrams of edible marijuana; ear plugs; earbuds; 60 dollars worth of groceries, including those that make it hardest for me to breathe (dairy, wheat)—but also Brussels sprouts, celery; 14 doses of Advair; 12 contact lenses; a minimal amount of water; toothpaste meant for children; more words than I can process, more words than I produce; 600 milligrams of Advil; images of ceilings, floors, faces; dust; few smells (too congested); tissues; no lotion (though my hands are cracking); cat fur (an accident); an unthinkable amount of germs; more blue light at night than doctors recommend; am I using *into* too liberally?; what about radio waves?; what about the 90-degree heat?; the ecolect of my cohort?; there is no word precise enough—eco meaning environment or house, idio meaning self, dia meaning through, between, across, and dialect referring to the language of a group, but never a group this small, and ethno meaning exactly what it sounds like, so I settle on eco, though I know what family feels like and this isn't it; though the tension here—based on ambiguously dirty looks, prosody, and what-they-meant-when-they-said—is easier than the more obvious aggression of my actual family; and I'll take what I can get anyway; *do you still talk to Ben?* my mother asks, as if a long-distance marriage isn't a marriage at all.

From Stein, "If I Told Him, A Completed Portrait of Picasso": Shutters shut and open so do queens. Shutters shut and shutters and so shutters shut and shutters and so and so shutters and so shutters shut and so shutters shut and shutters and so. And so shutters shut and so and also. And also and so and so and also.

Sometimes language can press down, too.

A coworker comes in at four. It's common for us to do trades on breaks, and I helped her out yesterday. I ask her to start on my lower back. She warms me up, sets down her ulna, the sharp edge of her forearm, and slides it off my iliac crest. She outlines my sacrum as if to teach me where it is. Through the sheet, she loosens my muscles by jostling me back and forth and digs into the gluteus minimus. I flinch. There are parts of the body that are almost never touched. As I get more comfortable, she slides her elbow into gluteus medius, a relief I can't express in words. Most people are hesitant to get this part of the body massaged, but they clench it and sit on it and work it out all day. She moves the bottoms of her palms and then her knuckles along gluteus maximus. It's common to cry when tension is released. I know I'll feel phantom fists still relaxing my muscles as I fall asleep tonight.

Stein on "loving repeating" from *The Making of Americans:*
As I was saying loving repeating being is in a way earthly being. In some it is repeating that gives to them always a solid feeling of being... Loving repeating in some is a going on always in them of earthly being, in some it is the way to completed understanding. Loving repeating then in some is their natural way of complete being.

About once a week—at times, once an hour—I still wonder if I should quit. Every time, I land on the same decision: no matter how much I miss my husband, there is something here worth exploring.

A man comes in at two. Agitated. But quickly his breathing becomes thick and steady. I've lulled him calm. Someone more mechanically inclined might work on the body as if it's a car. I work on his body like it's a poem. I'm hypnotized by the process. He's in pain, but he doesn't know where it's coming from. Referred pain shows up somewhere other than its source. There's something pleasing about a problem, not knowing the exact way out, but being confident in your ability to find it. About turning down the sound and getting out of your own way. You trace his scapulae, drawing two large triangles. They're riddled with knots, mostly lined up along the insides, with a few strays right below the inferior angle. It feels good to sink into them. To get lost in the rhythm, the manipulation of muscles, body on autopilot. When you stop thinking, you know what to do.

If loving repeating is complete being, what is loving breaking? I am not a self-destructive person. There's something about ambition that makes you split into smaller and smaller pieces. I don't regret being here. There's something about growth that makes you split into smaller and smaller pieces.

but the ghost of touch
                          language where hands should be

    that I'm already disjointed

Good Girl Through the Night

grinds her premonitions while
her lover stands in the doorway
sculpted, she matches

his energy and meaning, she cries
while he lowers the bricks

onto her legs though
she's asked him to—Jesus bleeding
through the pacifier

strangers bleeding in her bed
it's like leaves
it's like lavender—

starry night,
this is her usual bewilderment.

sorry night,
god drew her pitchfork spine.

Trouble

At a stoplight we discuss the finer points of religion.
Who would we spy on from heaven? If it were a place,
you'd choose the sexually depraved. *Some real nasty shit.*
You were soaked in loss. I wanted to dry you off.
In winter my skin starts to snake. A contrarian to the core,
you said you'd only want to argue with me.
Like *Lady and the Tramp,* a roller coaster begins
in your mouth, ends in mine.

HARDWIRED

My mother shrieks when she opens the door to my backyard. *What is that fucking thing?!* Anxious, I peer outside, try not to laugh. We're out of our element here in Texas. We're too wired. Still, even I know it's a deer.

To be fair, there are no such creatures in Queens and she rarely leaves her borough. Flying halfway across the country to see me involves a lot of emotional preparation and a couple of Xanax. My roommate's cat saunters into the yard. *Get him,* my mother pleads, grabbing my arm and squeezing with her acrylic nails. *It's gonna eat him.*

On the other hand, it's not like she's relaxed in the city. There's no shortage of predators there either. They lurk on side streets, in train cars, and in homes when mothers are at work. They disguise themselves as deliverymen, cable guys, and Jehovah's Witnesses. Like my mother, I'm hypervigilant. I'm an expert at tracking germs, words, and barely perceptible threats to my safety. Unlike my mother, I hide it pretty well. I remove her hand and let it drop.

A therapist asks what my anxiety would look like if it were a fictional character—a method for distancing oneself from one's emotions, often used with children. Mine is a nauseating shade of orange, with rubbery curved spikes and a nasty grin. The kind of cartoon character that would personify bacteria in a toothbrush commercial. He snarls his lip, taunting me.

That night I lie in bed, worrying about my depressed immune system and the patch of flaky skin on my upper arm, surrounded by an ominous red ring. A sensation is building in my lungs; something is crawling. It is relentless. I retrace my steps. First, I applied ointment, washed my hands, washed my hands again, and *then* I used my inhaler. Still, I wonder if fungal spores clung to the plastic and cannonballed down my pharynx. I imagine bright orange sea creatures blooming in my lungs. I want an invisible hand to gently crack open my rib cage and clear everything out, but I'm careful—if I close my eyes, I'll probably die. I know it's not strictly rational, but rational thoughts have no place in this climate. I write a note to my roommates, just in case I don't wake up. Something like: "It was the fungus."

My grandmother earned her anxiety. She raised six children by herself—three girls, three boys—on no income and no child support. Her youngest child, Victoria, required the most work and the most money. For a wheelchair, a ramp, medication, home attendants, a day-habilitation program, and an array of therapists. Things like privacy and some peace and quiet just weren't in the cards.

My mother earned her anxiety, too. She married a man she couldn't get along with; as she explains now, he paid for her dinners. The year she got divorced, we moved back in with my grandmother. My mother took care of her as she died of cancer, and then became Aunt Vicky's guardian. She also took care of my uncle every time he got out of Rikers Island, my great-grandparents in their last years, and of course, me and my sister. And still she managed to work full time.

I wonder if I've earned my anxiety or merely inherited it. I wonder if passing it on if or when I have children is inevitable, though now that I've turned thirty, everyone is more focused on the "when."

You have to crawl inside of your uncertainty and settle there. My advisor, Sima, always gives this advice. I'm in grad school, becoming a speech therapist. I keep making the same mistake—I'll spend an entire night doing a lesson plan for a one-hour session, and it all goes wrong anyway. *Follow the child's lead.* Her mantra. *Drop the plan. Adapt.* I'm in a session with four-year-old Thomas, trying to engage him. He tilts a toy back and forth in front of his eye, much too close for comfort, practically brushing up against his lashes. This is commonly referred to as "stimming" by therapists who aim to eliminate it, but Sima calls it self-regulation. *A child needs a sense of control.* I sit on the floor, facing him, and pretend the tiny car is fascinating me too. *Expand the schema.* I set the car on the racetrack and drive. Thomas watches. I recite *ready—set—go* and hope he'll drive too. But he is interested in other things. The sound of the wheels spinning, she explains, could be just as salient as the sound of my voice. He is processing things we don't even notice. He's wired differently. He knocks his head against the wall to a steady beat.

———

My earliest panic attacks are in kindergarten, where I spend most days in a bathroom stall. I'm not alone. In the Pepto-pink stall next to me, Abby Ludwig cries too. Out in the wild of the classroom, 48 other students run loose. The two teachers gossip in the corner. They have their limits, and extended bouts of crying (to say nothing of hyperventilating) are not allowed. They send us to our quiet zone, tell us to come out when we're ready to behave. But Abby and I spur each other on. Just as I think I'm feeling better, her wails scurry through my skin. I don't have to pee, but I zip, unzip, rezip my zipper to keep order, self-soothing, mad that the grownups had the gall to leave me in here.

———

I'm standing outside a sixth grader's locker. He's crouched inside of it and I'm trying to coax him out. *It's time to go to speech, Joseph.* I'm legally obligated to follow his Individualized Education Plan, whether he likes it or not. *I fucking hate you and I'm never coming to speech therapy again.* I think about walking away.

———

I'm in my speech room with a student in an early intervention center in the Bronx. He's almost five years old and can't talk yet, but that's not what we're working on. There are too many precursors to get to first. Joint attention, reciprocity. You can model language all you want, but if the child isn't tuned in, it'll be pointless. I try to engage him in a simple game, rolling a ball back and forth, but he throws it at me. He finds blocks and he throws those at me, too. He opens my toy closet and reaches for Mr. Potato Head, and Elefun, and I quickly lock the closet, berating myself for being stupid enough to leave it accessible in the first place, and try to move all hard objects into the hallway, careful to keep him from running out, and my cell phone keeps ringing, and I ignore it. I keep moving the hard objects, and I realize how futile this process is when he picks up the computer screen and chucks it at my head. I dodge it in time, sit down on the floor, and cry. He laughs, lacking "theory of mind," an ability to know how another person is feeling. For a second I put my face in my hands, and he climbs on the small table the other kids color on, bends his knees, and leaps onto me. Burnout for new teachers typically hits within three to five years. I wonder about the timeline for burnout in parenthood, and what you do when you can't quit. My cell phone rings again. In the throes of a panic attack, my mother texts: WHY WON'T YOU PICK UP? STOP DOING THIS TO ME.

———————

Ben is the first to help me see that there's a life I can live with fewer demands. The longest I go without speaking to my mother is six months, but it's a start. Soon I find weed, and soon I find Texas. A front porch where I can sit and think, look at deer. Soon I find writing, quit my day job. Soon I find marriage, a quiet space that I feel safe in.

———

Stoned, I love to be swaddled. I close my eyes to a symphony of impulse, to silence. Dumb as a statue. My cat scratches on my door, but I don't let her in. A wire-monkey mother. I realize my shoulders have been inching toward my ears all day. But now I'm alone. I touch all four walls, bask in the stillness of the room. Try not to wonder what marijuana does to my womb. No matter how much research I do, I never get the answer to my question: When do I need to stop in order to reverse the effects on my fertility? My husband thinks now would be a good time.

———

Biggest mistake of my life, Lorena mutters, as her son and daughter pull on her every limb, begging for something—more soda, or a pardon for not cleaning their rooms. I tutor them after school. Matthew is having a hard time in school because he erases everything he puts down. Christina has traumatic brain injury. She got it at a friend's house. She was horsing around when the parents weren't looking, and a light fixture fell on her head. She has trouble learning and remembering anything new, an unfortunate fate for a third-grader. *Never,* Lorena tells me, *and I mean never, have children. Don't even think about it.*

———

The biggest fight my mom and I ever had lasted the better part of a year. I told her I was getting my first tattoo, but she didn't believe it until she saw the fresh wound. Maybe she thought I'd be too scared to follow through. Every morning she greeted me with new ideas: *Have you tried washing it off? Rubbing Vitamin E on it? I bought this chemical online... If you scrape hard enough...* She stops just short of reaching for a cheese grater. Eventually she offers to pay thousands of dollars in laser removal. *Think about your choices,* she reminds me, though I had planned this for months. *Some mistakes are permanent.*

Children I have loved: Clara, a preschooler with a penchant for Elmo and asking me to cuddle. Henry, a fourth-grader with no regard for social skills but an endearing fascination with black holes. Mariya, who bites her classmates but feels so sorry for it afterward. She grew up in an understaffed orphanage in Russia. Her social worker tells me many students in her situation are misdiagnosed with autism, when the behavior actually stems from spending their early years detached from caretakers.

In 1958, Harry Harlow famously researched mother-infant bonds using rhesus monkeys. In his experiment, one mother monkey was made of wire and only provided food; another was covered in cloth and provided comfort. The infants consistently preferred cloth mothers, even when the variables were changed. In another study, monkeys were raised with only one or the other. Harlow found that the infants with wire mothers were psychologically stressed, sickly without the cloth. I wonder what kind of mother I'd be. A stereotypically overprotective mother; a pathologically enmeshed mother; a disconnected, depressed mother; a passing-for-normal mother. I guess being any kind of mother would entail getting out of this bed. I turn on the heating pad, tuck my blanket in on both sides.

———————

My direct supervisor looms over me. I imagine her to be twice my height (typical ten-foot-tall Midwestern woman) and twice my age. Late in the school year she mentions that she's 24—not twice my age but my exact age—and I feel conspicuously immature. My face, my voice, my work ethic. Nothing seems to be catching up. I'm an independent contractor at the elementary school. They don't have room for me, so they throw together a few solutions. Set up shop here, right next to the principal's desk. Try to act normal as she listens to your every word. Or share a room with the social worker; we'll throw HIPAA out the window. Not working out? How about a book closet? Dimly lit, crammed with excess *Velveteen Rabbits* and *Wild Things,* I settle in. Squeeze onto a tiny chair meant for a five-year-old. We still get walk-ins in the middle of therapy, but for the most part I have time to grow. Growing in front of other people has always been difficult for me.

My favorite classroom is down the hall. Kindergarten. When I pick up Wiley, I take a deep breath outside the door and try to hide my mother's tics. Twenty-five children and two teachers are in a meditative state. They're listening to mellow indie bands while they paint with their fingers. I tiptoe over to my student, Wiley, who shakes his head adamantly. He doesn't want to leave. His teacher, Odette, kneels to his level and touches his shoulder. She gives him a knowing look. He loves her. He can't help but acquiesce. I'm envious—not just of her quiet confidence and her cheekbones, which have a life of their own, but of the way worries seem to slide right off of her. She's unflappable. Something I work way too hard at being.

I'm sitting outside a museum next to a marble lion. I'm killing time on my phone while I wait for a friend and I come across a picture of two children, one I've now seen many times. Odette's children. I don't work with her anymore, but an old coworker posted it. The boy is getting big. He has an easy smile. His tiny teeth are perfectly aligned. The girl is just a few months, with a pink bow and cheeks like dough. It's captioned: *May they rest in peace.* Something sinks.

I take on Odette's grief for a moment until I wonder why her post is absent, and if she's okay. It must have been a car crash. Or a plane crash. They must have been with their father. I Google their names, not expecting to find anything. *Odette Phillips-Smith kills five-year-old son, four-month-old daughter; attempts suicide.*

The same photograph pops up. Travis and Violet drank their mother's grape juice, laced with poison. Odette sealed the windows shut, turned on the gas stove, and drowned the children in the bathtub. Slit her own wrists. Failed to die.

I call my mother but hang up when she asks more questions than I want to answer. I can't stop looking at Odette's face. Her cheekbones. Her sulfur smile. I lean on the marble lion at my side and cry. It doesn't even attempt to comfort me.

In my twenties, I sit on countless blue couches, zip, unzip, rezip my purse ad nauseum, until a therapist walks in. Even though I'm here to talk about anxiety, compulsions, and depression, part of me continues to hide it. The first day with a new therapist is always the worst. I ask for talk therapy; they suggest CBT. I ask for CBT; I'm told to take more walks. I start to wonder if they're somehow all on the same page, pushing me to practice giving up control, or if I just have a knack for finding incompetent therapists.

At 24, I have my first bout of baby fever. I frequent a forum called "clucky," where 1,150 women talk about their eggs. A friend tells me it will pass if I want it to, and it does. But at 26, the year my mother and I don't speak, it comes back. I'm broke, and my Ben is rational, so I wait it out again. *What is this really about?* he has the annoying habit of asking me. It's dawning on me that a mother-daughter bond is going to force itself on me, one way or another.

All my friends are becoming mothers—seven in the last year alone. I visit one of them, and watch her comfort her crying baby. *I got you,* she says as she cradles him. *You're safe.* I consider the ethics of this lie, and whether I'd be able to tell it. One day, won't he learn what's really out there?

On being fit to parent: A therapist sets up a medical evaluation. *It's only temporary,* she tells me. *If you want to stop at any point, just let me know.* But another therapist warns me that if I go on meds and then go off them, an application to adopt a child would most likely be denied. I check with an agency, and they tell me the opposite: If you want to adopt, you can't have taken anti-anxiety medication in the past two years. Similarly, doctors advise against: Being on anti-anxiety meds while pregnant. Going off anti-anxiety meds to get pregnant. And, obviously, self-medicating while pregnant. Common sense advises against: Letting mental illness run wild.

Maybe I'm not wired for this.

What about Aviva? I ask when my husband picks up the phone. Meaning innocent, springtime. We both favor Hebrew names, but we disagree on which ones.

That's my mom's middle name, he responds. For a second I can't believe how serendipitous it is, until he tells me that Ashkenazi Jews don't name babies after living relatives. *It's bad luck.* Innocent, springtime. Back to the drawing board.

Another friend's baby is splayed across the sofa. She coos and the grownups swoon over her. But I want to scoop her up, cover her limbs. She looks vulnerable. Exposed.

Ben and I play a secret game. We save it for really bad days. I make myself into a ball on his lap. He cradles and rocks me. *You're the baby,* he says, fulfilling a deep-down need. He is six feet tall but thin enough that some days he gets on my lap. *I'm the baby,* he requests, and I oblige.

Mothers have mothered for 200,000 years. Wait—that can't be right. I ask him to repeat the number. *If we're talking anatomically modern humans, yeah. 200,000 years. And if the average mother gave birth at 20—though I'm rounding way up here; it's probably much younger—you would be the 10,000th mother in your lineage.* One of Ben's special skills: helping me recognize when I'm *maybe* being myopic.

Writing appears to be cathartic, a new therapist tells me, *but that's only true if you can pack it up and put it away when you're done. Think of a lion.* I can already tell this will not be useful. *I'm sure you know what it means when an animal experiences a fight-or-flight reaction.* I nod my head, suppressing the urge to roll my eyes. We've all heard it before. *It sounds like you're in this reactive mode 24/7. When a lion is in this mode, he hunts, eats, or mates. Something physical to release the adrenaline. Then he rests. He doesn't just kick up the fear and sit with it.* I see where she's going with this. *Anxiety and depression are two sides of the same coin. Overstimulation wears you out, so your body forces you to take a break.* And it only feels *slightly* reductive. *Close out your writing, your phone calls with your mother, and anything else that's causing this reaction, with something physical, like jumping jacks, and something restful, like a shower. As you finish your writing routine, remind yourself to pack it up and put it away.* Okay, pretty sound advice—though it's only the tip of the iceberg. I'll probably make an appointment to see her again. As I leave, she hands me her card. *Remember,* she adds, *think of the lion.* But I picture the wrong one—marble, and unmoving.

Lullaby for the Nervous

1.

lately I've been hiring the moon
to spy on me in my sleep
just to make sure
I'm still there

2.

swanning my neck I squint
to better see her pepper milk
extend my tongue
think of lapping it up

3.

should it worry me that my pulse
is unwieldy? I've never lived in a country
where I didn't speak the language

4.

I write myself a letter: if you love anxiety so much,
why don't you marry it?

5.

me and anxiety: we walked
down the aisle at noon
to an empty room
we had friends
but we didn't want them there

I wore a beige bodysuit
she wore sequins
and fur just as
striking as the day
we met
high-heeled
we listened
to Morrissey
what difference
does it make

6.
once I heard hundreds
of years from now
people would trace
their digital lineage
back to us
the beginning
of a new world

7.
I ask myself
if the mattress
is teeming
with tadpoles
or maggots
what's so bad
about being made
out of sand?

8.
in *Cosmicomics*
Calvino's moon
is a wet dream
more celebrity
than spy
yes she shines

9.
in the morning
I'll gather
tree roots
with my spoons
sink my hands
into the mud

10.
in the morning
I'll still be here
in the morning
I'll be fine

AFTER NIGHTMARES: A CATALOG OF DREAMS ON 20MG OF CITALOPRAM

Week One

My brain is diced like onions; no one's eyes are tearing. The chunks of my white matter are tossed onto freshly washed lettuce. Glistening. They look like tofu. Mood: agreeable.

Week Two

An Adult Swim comedian walks by and jizzes directly onto my shirt. Twice. It's not sexual, or threatening, or anything really. Maybe a little funny. I'm riding an elephant—and a police truck on top of an elephant—soaring through the residential streets of my childhood. Thudding. If humans roamed these roads, they'd think it was an earthquake. But it's just us and the tigers. Fur shining. Gently sedated? They're running in our direction, but not with malice. Just giving their legs a stretch. Showing off their orange. Why not? My roommate's housecat is hit by a car. I fall to my knees and sob. My father, played by an Asian-American television actor, hugs me tight. I wake up happy. I liked that we were an "us."

Week Three

I'm locked in a room. I'm with Hillary Clinton. Protestors smash through the window. I don't want to talk about it.

Week Four

My husband is hoarding water. Gallons of it. The police are coming. He knows it's illegal, but he needs it, in case of the apocalypse. *Get rid of it,* I want to plead, but I sense his fear. I help him hide the evidence.

Week Five

I shower with all my friends. We're loving it. The droplets on our faces compel us to get closer. Everybody on Earth has green eyes. I can't believe I never noticed.

Week Six

The walls are closing in on me. The room is barely large enough to contain my bed. I would say it's a perfect night, but I don't want to jinx it.

Portrait of the Woman
as Pressure Phosphene

Press eyes for flashing lights. Portrait of the woman
as a trance. As the twinge of recognition—
it gets really comfortable in there.
As the holding of breath. As puncturing
a casing, ribs like grassy cliffs. She's ghost sick. Portrait
as hands strengthened by dirt. As solitary animal. As the slip
in a chorus line. Wind-up deer. She never gets caught
in headlights. Sets herself going—as arcade
claw machine. As hazardess. Thunder cover band.
Portrait of the woman as a revelation. I didn't hear what she said
but it convinced me. A portrait at all—
there's nothing left to sway. Portrait of the woman
as paradise world, as kelp, as marble on marble countertop.
As full moon. As falling? As nebulae, bottled, and bursting, as motion.

SENSE OF SELF [INACCURATE]

A body of thick metal rope. Eyes of ruby—that's a given.

Sprinkled with cinnamon. With turmeric.

My lipstick is empty iron capsules glued to my mouth.

I'm hung on my emotions like hooks in a coat closet.

And pain. A ladybug pill and a blanket of woodpeckers.

Red-bellied. I need water syringed into my muscles.

Butterflies fly out of my knuckles, and clay pigeons.

My name is Diane. My name is crumbling pillars of chalk.

My limbs are waxy petals, my face is caked in mud foundation, mud blush.

I roll muscles between my fingers like marbles. Words like chewing gum. My circuit board is showing.

I twitch like bunny whiskers. My face is a Georgia O'Keefe painting.

I hear the world in fists.

I'm too tired without a mask, and with one.

Tonight I crank my jaw like a jack-in-the-box.

A lightning flash I'm trying to catch. Loading. Loading.

My canopy lids. Is it safe to live inside a dream?

Take my hollyhock. Take my calla lily.

Some people are just afraid of what they are on the inside.

SELECTED TEXT FROM INTERNET THERAPY

(Week 1)

What brings you here?

several days / nearly every day / more than half the days

Danielle will find peace in her relationship with X
extremely difficult / yes / no

a powerless position

Danielle will find joy in writing again
fair / fair

Danielle will let go of guilt from her past
infrequently / not at all

Please complete this worksheet
feelings of worthlessness, diminished concentration

Thank you for sharing information about yourself

I'm so glad you reached out for help

(Weeks 2 through 6)

The illness thing is new.
Out of the blue... the doctors couldn't pinpoint...
I usually try to reason...
...having to touch everything in the room.

I can see how the sudden death...
a real way to know if this is over-the-top or just...
I'm sorry that is the case.

I'm out of patience.
I feel desperate to start...
...my needs so peripheral... if that's okay.

You have waited long enough...

Just checking in, how are you?

Just checking in, how are you feeling?
Just checking in, how are you, Danielle?
Feel free to reach out whenever.

(Week 7)

a panic attack
        (during a pap smear)

the whole thing
kind of looming over me

the first cycle of trying to conceive
a process rather than an event

can you walk me through the thoughts/feelings
when your muscles clench?

you're never fully in control

a trained doctor
has a moral and legal duty

but people do all kinds of shit
they're not supposed to

ramming into a brick wall
that same basic lack of trust

the speculum so cold
and silver and clangy

you could think someone's normal
and they could throw out all the rules

in traumatic events, we learn to not feel safe
here's something that could be beneficial in your case

―――――――――

(Weeks 8–10)

a few days
in a row   with no breaks

work I feel proud of
Kind of a tall order

The appeal for some(thing)   natural
that it's pulled me up—just the fact

that I'm taking care of myself

in   art
time to myself
without having to worry

a strong correlation   between our physical

and mental health

Some space

        maybe refreshed

(Film) Treatment

A woman, a pit of darkness.

She's wearing a pink blindfold, thick goggles over that, and a costume-store elephant nose. She's dancing. Her dress sways tick tock.

A giant black page is turned. Glued to it, fluttering butterfly wings.

A girl sleeping on the ground with her knee in the air, hovering near her chest.

Banging on an old, creaky safe with a magnifying glass.

A face, several feet tall, divided into top and bottom by a thick green line. Colored pencil. The face is translucent. Underneath the translucence, underneath the line, the real girl, pressing out, gasping for air.

My favorite cousin climbs inside a mechanical frog. She's going to get hit by a car.

A body tries to swing like a hammock; gets stuck inside a swamp of tomato sauce.

Walking up a wall, getting stuck in glue.

An airplane in a hangar: The wall is washed with a paintbrush, and as it's washed it comes brick. Brick and baby blue in the shape of a plane. The wall around it still black.

Play means I'm calm. Or: Play makes me calm. They say retreating doesn't solve any problems, but it does.

She lifts a facsimile from the brick and flies away inside it.

ABOUT THE AUTHOR

Danielle Zaccagnino is an essayist, a poet, and an English teacher. She was the winner of *Sonora Review's* Essay Prize (2016) and Salem College's Rita Dove Prize in Poetry (2017). She has an MFA from Texas State University. Her writing appears in journals such as *Diagram, Waxwing, Sonora Review, and Puerto del Sol.* She is from Queens, New York.

ACKNOWLEDGMENTS

I'm grateful for everyone who helped this book come together, including:

my Texas State mentors: Cecily Parks, Debra Monroe, Cyrus Cassells, and Steve Wilson,

my cohort, especially Michaela, Meg, Micah, Laura, Jacob, Emily, Jeff, Graham, Tim, & Steven,

my family,

my AX teaching team,

the MJP team,

my oldest friends: Maureen, Sara, Britta,

Ben, for a decade of feedback and support,

Jack, for being my motherfucker,

and the journals who have published this work: *DIAGRAM, Waxwing, Sonora Review, The Butter, Puerto del Sol, Rust + Moth, Story | Houston, Day One, Gravel, The Boiler,* & *Word Riot.*

Other Title From Mason Jar Press

The Horror is Us
an anthology of horror fiction edited by Justin Sanders

Ashley Sugarnotch & the Wolf
poems by Elizabeth Deanna Morris Lakes

…and Other Disasters
short stories by Malka Older

Manhunt
a novella by Jaime Fountaine

The Couples
a novella by Nicole Callihan

All Friends Are Necessary
a novella by Tomas Moniz

Continental Breakfast
poetry by Danny Caine

How to Sit
memoir by Tyrese Coleman

Broken Metropolis
an anthology of queer speculative fiction edited by Dave Ring

Learn more at masonjarpress.com